THE PATH OF AN ACHIEVER

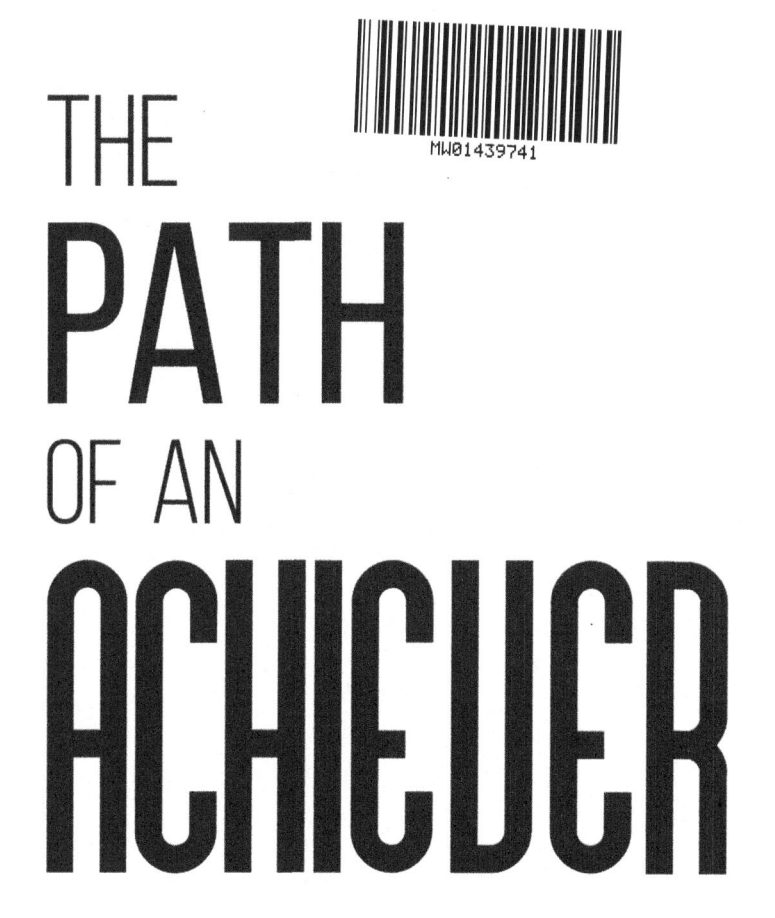

FRANCIS B. THOMAS

Copyright ©2023 Francis B. Thomas

All Scripture quotations are taken from
the New King James Version unless otherwise stated.

All rights reserved solely by the author. The author guarantees that the contents of this book do not infringe on the rights of any person or work. No portion of this book may be reproduced mechanically, electronically or by any other means, without the written permission of the author.

For copies, please visit: www.womanonpurpose.org
or your online book store.

ISBN: 9798395378842
Published by

mproved
...the improved you

www.improved2life.com

To Contact the Author
Bishop Francis B. Thomas
World Resurrection Ministries Inc.
4117 Woerner Avenue
Levittown, PA 19057
Phone: 267-709-0723
Email: francisbthomas@yahoo.com

TABLE OF CONTENTS

Introduction 1

Chapter One: The Pregnancy 7

Chapter Two: Interpretation of the Vision 23

Chapter Three: The Right Environment 33

Chapter Four: The Role of a Mentor 41

Chapter Five: The Place of Sacrifice 47

Chapter Six: The Pitfalls 57

Chapter Seven: Laser Focus 69

Conclusion 73

THE PATH OF AN ACHIEVER

INTRODUCTION

As I sat in my car, I pondered over the day's weather report. This summer is going to be very hot. I drove into the already messy traffic of Cottman Avenue. It is Friday, and it is scorched. I was on my way to pick my daughter up from school. It should have taken me fifteen minutes, but I am in the twentieth minute and still not there yet. I noticed the presence of police cars on the road; there had been an accident. I finally drove to the school, where she was waiting. Unlike every other day, her demeanor was different. I asked how school was that day, and she told me she had been attacked by two of her schoolmates. I asked her what had happened. She told me that she had been commended earlier in class that day for stepping up and doing better than everyone in their class. She was very happy, but not everyone was happy. She told me how after their lunch break, she was attacked by her two classmates, telling her, "Who do you think you are?" I asked what she did after the incident, but she said nothing. I inquired whether her teacher was aware of the incident, and she said yes, adding that she had laid a formal complaint.

She then asked me why people are jealous and hateful in life. I wasn't expecting that question, and it took me unaware from a sixth grader. I told her that is the depraved part of human nature that we must all live with. I also told her that it is a distraction she will face

INTRODUCTION

as she grows up. I became a teacher at that moment, instructing her to be ready to pay the price of becoming an achiever. Every achievement will be intimidating to many non-achievers. The fact that you had an achievement in any endeavor of life is a message to others who did the same thing and did not succeed that you are better off and they are losers. I knew this was strange to her, but I took time to tell her some reality of life.

The biggest conduit for success and achieving your goal is never to be distracted. There are many today who should have been at the top of their game but got distracted because they were offended. To become an achiever, you must be willing to fight, to scratch with inner tenacity and audacity. To be an achiever, there must be a part that you thread. To be an achiever, there is a place that you must walk through. Whatever area of life you find yourself in, your focus should be on achieving that goal. However, to achieve that goal, you must possess a few principles. Achievements have a requisite; therefore, we must locate that quality and go for it. What does it mean to achieve, or how can we define achievement? Achievement is a thing done successfully, typically by effort, courage, or skill. It is the process of achieving something. Achievement denotes accomplishing a task. It will take some effort to accomplish any task in life. Success doesn't just come; it is made to happen.

The man with the greatest success that ever lived was Jesus. In order to accomplish His mission of salvation

INTRODUCTION

for humanity, Jesus marched like the champion that He is to the cross of Calvary to lay down His life for humanity. The writer of the Book of Hebrew says we must look on to Jesus, the author and the finisher of our faith, who, for the joy that was set before Him, endured the shame of the cross. In this book, we will study Jesus Christ and explore His achievement story as our great example. Achievement is a spirit. It is my prayer that as you read this book, you will be able to contact that Spirit so that in all your endeavors in life, you can record achievement galore. Over the years, I have taken my time to study great men and women around the world, and they seem to have many things in common. We are also going to explore them in this book so that we might learn what they know.

THE PATH OF AN ACHIEVER

CHAPTER ONE

THE PREGNANCY

If you are going to be an achiever, you must first know where you are going and identify where you are not going. You can't go anywhere without knowing where you are going. An achiever is one who knows what they want and knows how to get it. To achieve is to get it done. Vision is a keyword for an achiever. Vision is the ability to picture the future. The word of God declares that without vision, the people will perish. Whatever you can't see, you can't access, and whatever you can't see, you can't seize. Whatever you want to become in life, you have to envision it.

Vision is like pregnancy; it is an incubated baby in the womb. Vision is birthed from the womb of the Spirit with the activity of the mind. In the book of Genesis, we were introduced to the story of creation. What we must understand about the creation story is the fact that God was pregnant before He started giving birth to creation. So if there was anything like Genesis chapter one verse zero, it would be God was pregnant. God is an achiever. He achieved the feat of placing this planet in its place. Everything that God made was inside God before it was made.

THE PREGNANCY

Genesis 1, King James Version (KJV)

> **1** In the beginning God created the Heaven and the earth.
>
> **2** And the earth was without form, and void; and darkness was upon the face of the deep. And the Spirit of God moved upon the face of the waters.
>
> **3** And God said, Let there be light: and there was light.
>
> **4** And God saw the light, that it was good: and God divided the light from the darkness.
>
> **5** And God called the light Day, and the darkness he called Night. And the evening and the morning were the first day.
>
> **6** And God said, Let there be a firmament in the midst of the waters, and let it divide the waters from the waters.

7 And God made the firmament, and divided the waters which were under the firmament from the waters which were above the firmament: and it was so.

8 And God called the firmament Heaven. And the evening and the morning were the second day.

9 And God said, Let the waters under the Heaven be gathered together unto one place, and let the dry land appear: and it was so.

10 And God called the dry land earth; and the gathering together of the waters called he Seas: and God saw that it was good.

11 And God said, Let the earth bring forth grass, the herb yielding seed, and the fruit tree yielding fruit after his kind, whose seed is in itself, upon the earth: and it was so.

THE PREGNANCY

12 And the earth brought forth grass, and herb yielding seed after his kind, and the tree yielding fruit, whose seed was in itself, after his kind: and God saw that it was good.

13 And the evening and the morning were the third day.

14 And God said, Let there be lights in the firmament of the Heaven to divide the day from the night; and let them be for signs, and for seasons, and for days, and years:

15 And let them be for lights in the firmament of the Heaven to give light upon the earth: and it was so.

16 And God made two great lights; the greater light to rule the day, and the lesser light to rule the night: he made the stars also.

17 And God set them in the firmament of the Heaven to give light upon the earth,

18 And to rule over the day and over the night, and to divide the light from the darkness: and God saw that it was good.

19 And the evening and the morning were the fourth day.

20 And God said, Let the waters bring forth abundantly the moving creature that hath life, and fowl that may fly above the earth in the open firmament of Heaven.

21 And God created great whales, and every living creature that moveth, which the waters brought forth abundantly, after their kind, and every winged fowl after his kind: and God saw that it was good.

22 And God blessed them, saying, Be fruitful, and multiply, and fill the waters in the seas, and let fowl multiply in the earth.

23 And the evening and the morning were the fifth day.

24 And God said, Let the earth bring forth the living creature after his kind, cattle, and creeping thing, and beast of the earth after his kind: and it was so.

25 And God made the beast of the earth after his kind, and cattle after their kind, and every thing that creepeth upon the earth after his kind: and God saw that it was good.

26 And God said, Let us make man in our image, after our likeness: and let them have dominion over the fish of the sea, and over the fowl of the air, and over the cattle, and over all the earth, and over every creeping thing that creepeth upon the earth.

> **27** So God created man in his own image, in the image of God created he him; male and female created he them.
>
> **28** And God blessed them, and God said unto them, Be fruitful, and multiply, and replenish the earth, and subdue it: and have dominion over the fish of the sea, and over the fowl of the air, and over every living thing that moveth upon the earth.

Everything we see in this text is tied to the vision that God had from the beginning. The account in this text tells us that the Spirit of God moved upon the face of the waters. The movement of God is in the vision of God. We are also made in the image of God. If we are going to be great achievers like God, we must be men and women with vision. We must become pregnant like God. We are His imagery on this planet, and if we continue in our capacity as His administrator of the earth, we must be vision-minded and ready to work it through. That is why any man or woman with no vision of where they are going is definitely not going anywhere. Many of the giants and heroes of the Bible were men of vision. It is also fascinating to know that God worked with them on what they could see. The only thing that kept Abraham going in the Bible was the fact that he could see. He could have been overwhelmed by discouragement and unbelief, but he kept on seeing until he was able to seize.

Genesis 15:1-6, King James Version (KJV)

> **1** After these things the word of the Lord came unto Abram in a vision, saying, Fear

not, Abram: I am thy shield, and thy exceeding great reward.

2 And Abram said, Lord God, what wilt thou give me, seeing I go childless, and the steward of my house is this Eliezer of Damascus?

3 And Abram said, Behold, to me thou hast given no seed: and, lo, one born in my house is mine heir.

4 And, behold, the word of the Lord came unto him, saying, This shall not be thine heir; but he that shall come forth out of thine own bowels shall be thine heir.

5 And he brought him forth abroad, and said, Look now toward Heaven, and tell the stars, if thou be able to number them: and he said unto him, So shall thy seed be.

> **6** And he believed in the Lord; and he counted it to him for righteousness

Abraham, against all hope, believed because vision was involved. What he saw became the conduit and the energy of his miracle. The vision became his shock absorber. This was not just limited to Abraham; it was evident in all who God called. God will sometimes ask them what they saw. He asked Jeremiah what he saw, and Jeremiah said I saw an almond tree. He told him He would watch over His word to perform it. We must never forget that our achievement is tied to what we can see. In the school of God, no one is permitted to enter into what they can't see. It is my prayer that God will open our eyes to see where God is taking us.

There are different kinds of vision and pregnancy. However, the durability of every vision and pregnancy is tied to its source. Whenever God gives you a vision, or so to speak, a pregnancy, you can rest assured that it is guaranteed. Why? Because He that gives the vision also has the capability for its fulfillment. The perfect way of being impregnated by God is to develop a relationship with him. This is very significant. It is your relationship with God that caused a vision or pregnancy to be borne in your heart. Apostle Paul's declaration in the book of Philippians is fascinating.

Philippians 3:10-12, King James Version (KJV)

> **10** That I may know him, and the power of his resurrection, and the fellowship of his

> sufferings, being made conformable unto his death;
>
> **11** If by any means I might attain unto the resurrection of the dead.
>
> **12** Not as though I had already attained, either were already perfect: but I follow after, if that I may apprehend that for which also I am apprehended of Christ Jesus.

When Paul used the words 'that I may know him', it was synonymous with the same knowing we see between a husband and wife. For example, Adam knew his wife, Noah knew his wife, and Isaac knew his wife. So what Paul was saying was very romantic in nature. He was describing the love between a groom and his bride. It is a love affair between a man and his wife. Paul was deeper in this text than we see. The knowing of God is that of intimacy. In normal life, the intimacy of a man is what results in pregnancy. So also, if we are in intimacy with the Holy Spirit, we will be impregnated with visions and dreams. We must never forget that Jesus is our groom, and we are the bride. The book of Revelation admonishes us. Let us rejoice and shout for joy! Let us give Him glory *and* honor, for the marriage of the Lamb has come at last, and His bride the redeemed has prepared herself. She has been permitted to dress in fine linen, dazzling white and clean, for the fine linen signifies the righteous acts of the saints, the ethical conduct, personal integrity, moral courage, and godly character of believers.

We are the bride of the Lamb. If we are the bride of Christ, then we must know that every intimacy with the groom is a great opportunity for pregnancy or vision. If we are going to be achievers, we must develop our relationship with God. It must be paramount to us. Our relationship with God is more important than the work we are doing for God. If we are determined to achieve, we must know what we want. Vision is that conduit we need to navigate through what we want to achieve. It is my prayer we will delve into a deeper relationship that will produce great vision in our lives.

THE PATH OF AN ACHIEVER

CHAPTER TWO

INTERPRETATION OF THE VISION

Having a vision of where you are going is very important. However, if you can't interpret your vision, it will remain in the dark. If you keep having visions about what you want to do and do nothing about it, you might end up forgetting about it. To interpret your vision is to seek an understanding of what you are seeing. Every vision has a time span, and it is very important to know how to go about making your vision a reality. Many people have visions of where they are going but do nothing about it. I have seen many people with great visions of bettering their world. This vision never transformed into reality because they didn't do anything about it. If you are going to be an achiever, you must consciously sit down and go to work by setting a strategy. You must have a strategy for taking it from the realm of just vision to reality. We must never forget that nothing works until you work it. When you have a vision of what you want to achieve, don't go to sleep but rather go to work.

Sometimes visions could be synonymous with dreams. We can have a dream about what we want to achieve, but we must do all we can to interpret the dream and how to accomplish it. In the case of Joseph in the Old Testament, he was not just a dreamer but also an

INTERPRETATION OF THE VISION

interpreter. King Pharaoh had a dream about how to achieve a land of surplus in a time of famine that was coming. In all of his dreams, he could not interpret them. Pharaoh's achievement is tied to his ability to interpret his dreams. Come to think about it, Pharaoh had a dream of what must be achieved in his tenure but simply had no idea what to do because he couldn't interpret his own dream.

Genesis 41:14-40, King James Version (KJV)

> **14** Then Pharaoh sent and called Joseph, and they brought him hastily out of the dungeon: and he shaved himself, and changed his raiment, and came in unto Pharaoh.
>
> **15** And Pharaoh said unto Joseph, I have dreamed a dream, and there is none that can

interpret it: and I have heard say of thee, that thou canst understand a dream to interpret it.

16 And Joseph answered Pharaoh, saying, It is not in me: God shall give Pharaoh an answer of peace.

17 And Pharaoh said unto Joseph, In my dream, behold, I stood upon the bank of the river:

18 And, behold, there came up out of the river seven kine, fatfleshed and well favoured; and they fed in a meadow:

19 And, behold, seven other kine came up after them, poor and very ill favoured and leanfleshed, such as I never saw in all the land of Egypt for badness:

20 And the lean and the ill favoured kine did eat up the first seven fat kine:

INTERPRETATION OF THE VISION

21 And when they had eaten them up, it could not be known that they had eaten them; but they were still ill favoured, as at the beginning. So I awoke.

22 And I saw in my dream, and, behold, seven ears came up in one stalk, full and good:

23 And, behold, seven ears, withered, thin, and blasted with the east wind, sprung up after them:

24 And the thin ears devoured the seven good ears: and I told this unto the magicians; but there was none that could declare it to me.

25 And Joseph said unto Pharaoh, The dream of Pharaoh is one: God hath shewed Pharaoh what he is about to do.

26 The seven good kine are seven years; and the seven good ears are seven years: the dream is one.

27 And the seven thin and ill favoured kine that came up after them are seven years; and the seven empty ears blasted with the east wind shall be seven years of famine.

28 This is the thing which I have spoken unto Pharaoh: What God is about to do he sheweth unto Pharaoh.

29 Behold, there come seven years of great plenty throughout all the land of Egypt:

30 And there shall arise after them seven years of famine; and all the plenty shall be forgotten in the land of Egypt; and the famine shall consume the land;

INTERPRETATION OF THE VISION

31 And the plenty shall not be known in the land by reason of that famine following; for it shall be very grievous.

32 And for that the dream was doubled unto Pharaoh twice; it is because the thing is established by God, and God will shortly bring it to pass.

33 Now therefore let Pharaoh look out a man discreet and wise, and set him over the land of Egypt.

34 Let Pharaoh do this, and let him appoint officers over the land, and take up the fifth part of the land of Egypt in the seven plenteous years.

35 And let them gather all the food of those good years that come, and lay up corn under the hand of Pharaoh, and let them keep food in the cities.

36 And that food shall be for store to the land against the seven years of famine, which shall be in the land of Egypt; that the land perish not through the famine.

37 And the thing was good in the eyes of Pharaoh, and in the eyes of all his servants.

38 And Pharaoh said unto his servants, Can we find such a one as this is, a man in whom the Spirit of God is?

39 And Pharaoh said unto Joseph, Forasmuch as God hath shewed thee all this, there is none so discreet and wise as thou art:

40 Thou shalt be over my house, and according unto thy word shall all my people be ruled: only in the throne will I be greater than thou.

INTERPRETATION OF THE VISION

In this text, Pharaoh was frightened by what he saw. He knew that he had a mission to achieve betterment for his people, but he had to be able to interpret his dreams. Unfortunately, his wise men and counselors could not help him until his attention was drawn to Joseph by an ex-convict who was an inmate alongside Joseph in prison. This was the butler that Joseph helped by interpreting his dream with his friend, the baker. Joseph was brought forth, and he eventually interpreted the dream of Pharaoh. Historical records tell us the greatness of the Pharaoh at that time was attributed to Joseph.

According to Josephus, the Jewish historian, one of the times when Joseph might have been in Egypt could have been during the Middle Kingdom, 2000 BC to 1786 BC.

Joseph might have come to Egypt during the reign of Sesostris II (1894 BC-1878 BC). Since he achieved his position at the court of the king some years after having been brought to Egypt, Joseph would have served under Sesostris III (1878 BC -1841 BC). Sesostris III was a noted warrior, greatly expanding Egypt's territory through the conquest of Nubia. He instituted administrative reforms which reduced the power of the nobility. Joseph lived in Egypt for 71 years, so Joseph died in approximately 1805 BC, under the reign of Amenemhet III (1841 BC-1797 BC). In the reign of Sesostris III, Egypt became prosperous because Joseph interpreted Pharaoh's dream. Our achievement will be guaranteed once we have a vision or a dream of where we are going and we are able to interpret it.

CHAPTER THREE

THE RIGHT ENVIRONMENT

The path of an achiever is made clear in the choice of their environment. Every progress is often determined by the environment and the atmosphere they are in. Growth is guaranteed mostly by the environment. For example, fish can only grow while in the water. If you take them out of the water, they will stop growing and eventually die. Likewise, if you take a plant from its soil environment, it will stop growing and eventually die. The reason is simple; God has set ordinances for the growth of everything based on the source of its environment.

If you have a vision of what you want to achieve, you must choose your environment wisely. You must choose the environment that will help your vision to grow. Like the case of a pregnant woman, she must maintain a certain environment so that she will avoid a miscarriage. She must go to the right hospital to help her pregnancy grow the right way. A man or woman who wants to accomplish their vision must be conscious of their environment. You must surround yourself with places that can challenge you to do better and be in an environment that can cheer you up to go for it. You must surround yourself with encouragers and, at the same time, those who can correct you when you are going off

THE RIGHT ENVIRONMENT

course. You must choose your working environment wisely. For example, you must choose the type of job that will build your vision and career. You must engage in the type of business that will align with your vision and your dream. You must enroll in a school that is patterned after your goals and aspirations. To be a great achiever, you must pay attention to these details.

The path of an achiever is carved by who they surround themselves with. The Church that you go to is also significant to your growth. Every Bible-believing Church is good, but not every Church is good for you. Staying in a certain Church might affect your vision negatively. Staying in a certain Church might derail from the right course. Likewise, being in the right Church could be a plus for your vision. Being in the right Church can be of great benefit to your achievement in life. Being in a Church that can challenge the potential on your inside could be a catalyst for your achievement. Interestingly as a believer, God will lead you to the environment that will be a blessing to the place where He is taking you. God will often take you to an environment that challenges you to improve.

Jesus was clear about His mission from the beginning. At the age of twelve, He was in the temple, engaging the rabbis in what will help Him achieve His goals. At thirty, God led Him into the wilderness. He led Him to the environment that would prepare Him properly for what He was about to accomplish.

THE RIGHT ENVIRONMENT

Luke 4:1-14, King James Version (KJV)

> **1** And Jesus being full of the Holy Ghost returned from Jordan, and was led by the Spirit into the wilderness,
>
> **2** Being forty days tempted of the devil. And in those days he did eat nothing: and when they were ended, he afterward hungered.
>
> **3** And the devil said unto him, If thou be the Son of God, command this stone that it be made bread.
>
> **4** And Jesus answered him, saying, It is written, That man shall not live by bread alone, but by every word of God.
>
> **5** And the devil, taking him up into an high mountain, shewed unto him all the kingdoms of the world in a moment of time.
>
> **6** And the devil said unto him, All this power will I give thee, and the glory of them: for that

is delivered unto me; and too whomsoever I will I give it.

7 If thou therefore wilt worship me, all shall be thine.

8 And Jesus answered and said unto him, Get thee behind me, Satan: for it is written, Thou shalt worship the Lord thy God, and him only shalt thou serve.

9 And he brought him to Jerusalem, and set him on a pinnacle of the temple, and said unto him, If thou be the Son of God, cast thyself down from hence:

10 For it is written, He shall give his angels charge over thee, to keep thee:

11 And in their hands they shall bear thee up, lest at any time thou dash thy foot against a stone.

> **12** And Jesus answering said unto him, It is said, Thou shalt not tempt the Lord thy God.
>
> **13** And when the devil had ended all the temptation, he departed from him for a season.
>
> **14** And Jesus returned in the power of the Spirit into Galilee: and there went out a fame of him through all the region round about.

This wilderness was the perfect environment for the goal that was set before Him. This environment helped Him in His vision as He learned how to overcome. This wilderness experience was the conduit to the success He accomplished on the cross of Calvary. The writer of the book of Luke makes us understand that after the wilderness experience, His fame spread throughout the region. Every man or woman of vision must be careful about the type of friends they surround themselves with. They must surround themselves with like-minded people. If you keep hanging out with those who are not going anywhere, you will soon forget where you are going. It is my prayer that you will choose your environment wisely.

CHAPTER FOUR

THE ROLE OF A MENTOR

Whatever you are trying to achieve, someone has achieved something similar. All you need to do is identify this person and learn their path. No star suddenly becomes a star; every star is a product of another star, just like the moon is a reflection of the sun. No matter where you are going, someone has traveled that road before. Your assignment is to identify that person and connect with them. Every achiever needs a mentor. There are people who are unique to where you are going and your life journey. Mentorship is a relationship in which a more experienced or more knowledgeable person helps to guide a less experienced or less knowledgeable person. The mentor may be older or younger than the person being mentored, but they must have a certain area of expertise. It is a learning and development partnership between someone with vast experience and someone who wants to learn. Interaction with an expert may also be necessary to gain proficiency.

Every achiever must meticulously select a mentor that is compatible with their area of specialization. By so doing, they will be in a better position to do better in their field. In the books of the Bible, God sets up systems of mentorship that we can pattern ourselves after. We see how Moses mentored Joshua for the mantle of leadership.

Deuteronomy 31:22-24, King James Version (KJV)

> **22** Moses therefore wrote this song the same day, and taught it the children of Israel.
>
> **23** And he gave Joshua the son of Nun a charge, and said, Be strong and of a good courage: for thou shalt bring the children of Israel into the land which I sware unto them: and I will be with thee.
>
> **24** And it came to pass, when Moses had made an end of writing the words of this law in a book, until they were finished,

Deuteronomy 34:7-9, King James Version (KJV)

> **7** And Moses was an hundred and twenty years old when he died: his eye was not dim, nor his natural force abated.

> **8** And the children of Israel wept for Moses in the plains of Moab thirty days: so the days of weeping and mourning for Moses were ended.
>
> **9** And Joshua the son of Nun was full of the spirit of wisdom; for Moses had laid his hands upon him: and the children of Israel hearkened unto him, and did as the Lord commanded Moses.

We also see how Elisha had a monumental achievement because he had a great mentorship from Elijah. As a matter of fact, Elisha did twice what Elijah did in his days. Jesus spent three years of His life mentoring His disciples. No wonder when Jesus left, the achievements of His disciples were colossal. In the New Testament, we also see how Apostle Paul mentored Timothy. To arrive at great feats in our pursuit of achievements, we must not negate the place of mentorship. The acts of mentorship are like a vehicle that takes you to the port of achievement. There will be a painstaking on the part of the mentee to follow through with his mentor so he can benefit from the wells of experience that the mentor is having. It will also take humility to submit to the mentor, which grants the mentee access to the mentor.

You can access mentorship from one-on-one relationships. You can also receive mentorship through books and tapes. Whatever it might be, make sure you have a mentor in your life to help you achieve your goals. Find someone who can speak to your life, teach, encourage, and correct you. A mentor could be your Pastor, school teacher, coach, or CEO. Whoever that person might be, we must pay attention to him so that we can reap the benefit of it all. It is my prayer that God will bless you with a good mentor.

CHAPTER FIVE

THE PLACE OF SACRIFICE

The path of an achiever is also the path of sacrifice. For you to achieve your goal, there is a place of sacrifice that will be inescapable. Everyone that ever became an achiever made some sacrifice to be there. In every endeavor of life, if we must come to a place of prominence, we must be willing to make some level of sacrifice. What is sacrifice? A sacrifice is an act of giving up something valued for the sake of something else regarded as more important or worthy. We all must make sacrifices if we are going to make progress. The amount of sacrifice we are willing to make will determine how far we can go. The place of sacrifice is the place of success, power, and achievement.

Once we have a vision of where we are going, there will be different types of things clamoring for our attention. However, we have to decide what is our priority. We have to decide where we are leaning on. There are many people who started very well; they had a vision of where they were going, they could interpret the vision, and they had the right environment and the right mentor, but they were not willing to make the sacrifice to get to where they are going in life. Listen, success and great achievement will cost you something. If you are not willing to let go of some distractions, you may not amount to anything. To make a sacrifice is to have the doggedness to move on in the midst of many challenges. To make a sacrifice is to stay awake while others are sleeping to tend to your goal. To make a sacrifice is to leave the minor and focus on the major things. Even when the odds are against you, you can square your shoulder and pursue your goal. To make a sacrifice is to rise up and fight even when it is not convenient. Every achiever is often marked by many scars of their battle for success. Only achievers and champions make sacrifices. It may not be convenient, but they make sacrifices. They may not be well in their body, but they make sacrifices. They may not have the money, but they make sacrifices. They don't make excuses. They go ahead and make the necessary sacrifice to achieve their goal.

The stories of the Bible are filled with men and women who made enormous sacrifices for where they were going. Their God Himself was the God of sacrifice. There were great men and women of sacrifice. Their heart towards sacrifice was what separated them from others. It seems clear that the place of sacrifice is where God knows your heart towards your goal. When God called Abraham, he cooperated with God by leaving present-day Syria to where God was sending him. But when it came to a time when God would finally cut a covenant of magnitude achievement with him, He tested him by asking him to sacrifice his only son.

THE PLACE OF SACRIFICE

Genesis 22:1-14, King James Version (KJV)

> **1** And it came to pass after these things, that God did tempt Abraham, and said unto him, Abraham: and he said, Behold, here I am.
>
> **2** And he said, Take now thy son, thine only son Isaac, whom thou lovest, and get thee into the land of Moriah; and offer him there for a burnt offering upon one of the mountains which I will tell thee of.
>
> **3** And Abraham rose up early in the morning, and saddled his ass, and took two of his young men with him, and Isaac his son, and clave the wood for the burnt offering, and rose up, and went unto the place of which God had told him.
>
> **4** Then on the third day Abraham lifted up his eyes, and saw the place afar off.

5 And Abraham said unto his young men, Abide ye here with the ass; and I and the lad will go yonder and worship, and come again to you.

6 And Abraham took the wood of the burnt offering, and laid it upon Isaac his son; and he took the fire in his hand, and a knife; and they went both of them together.

7 And Isaac spake unto Abraham his father, and said, My father: and he said, Here am I, my son. And he said, Behold the fire and the wood: but where is the lamb for a burnt offering?

8 And Abraham said, My son, God will provide himself a lamb for a burnt offering: so they went both of them together.

9 And they came to the place which God had told him of; and Abraham built an altar there, and laid the wood in order, and bound Isaac his son, and laid him on the altar upon the wood.

10 And Abraham stretched forth his hand, and took the knife to slay his son.

11 And the angel of the Lord called unto him out of Heaven, and said, Abraham, Abraham: and he said, Here am I.

12 And he said, Lay not thine hand upon the lad, neither do thou any thing unto him: for now I know that thou fearest God, seeing thou hast not withheld thy son, thine only son from me.

13 And Abraham lifted up his eyes, and looked, and behold behind him a ram caught in a thicket by his horns: and Abraham went and took the ram, and offered him up for a burnt offering in the stead of his son.

> **14** And Abraham called the name of that place Jehovahjireh: as it is said to this day, In the mount of the Lord it shall be seen

The place of sacrifice became the altar used as a determinate factor. God demanded Isaac from Abraham, and Abraham went ahead in the test of achievement by sacrificing his son. Even though God replaced the life of Isaac with a ram, it was clear that Abraham had made up his mind and had technically killed Isaac before the angel of the Lord stopped him. Think about it, if you reach the place of sacrifice, it is a sign that you have already achieved. It is fascinating to note that God was determined to bring salvation to humanity in the new testament. His plan was to bring redemption to humanity. From the Old Testament, He sent the law and later the prophets, but they could not achieve this feat of salvation. God decided the only way to achieve this would be by way of sacrifice. The book of John, chapter three, verse sixteen, declares that God so loved the world that He gave His only begotten son, that whosoever believes in Him will not perish but have everlasting life. God made the ultimate sacrifice by giving His only son. Abraham was also willing to give his son. The result was outstanding. Sacrifice never fails. The achievement of salvation was made possible through the sacrifice of the blood of Jesus Christ.

If we are going to achieve our goals and visions in life, we must be willing to make the necessary sacrifice that will make us graduate with flying colors in the school of achievement. It is my prayer that God will grant us the grace to make the necessary sacrifice for every move we make towards achievement.

CHAPTER SIX

THE PITFALLS

There are pitfalls in the path of an achiever. Every achiever must find out the forbidden fruit that they need to pay attention to. Every would-be achiever must find out the hidden landmines and stumbling blocks that might hinder them from achieving their goals. Pitfalls are unsuspected difficulties or dangers. Pitfalls denote danger, difficulty, peril, traps, and hazards that are hidden that we can't easily see. Some things are injurious to our achievement, and we must pay attention to them. There are many people today who did not achieve their goals or turn their vision into reality because they underestimated and overlooked certain things. If you refuse to pay attention to the pitfalls surrounding you, you might end up paying a great price.

You must first avoid certain friends that are not healthy for where you are going. You must also avoid being in the wrong company of people with no ambition of making progress with their lives. If you tarry in the company of those who are not going anywhere, you can easily be choked up. As an illustration, I described vision as being like pregnancy in this book. If a pregnant woman does not listen to the advice of her doctor about her pitfalls, she might have a miscarriage. Similarly,

THE PITFALLS

anyone with a vision who does not pay attention to the pitfalls of life might also have a miscarriage. To have a spiritual miscarriage is to fall by the wayside without achieving what God has called them to do. As we advance with the journey of life, we must pay attention to those things that might want us to trip.

However, we must not forget that there will be challenges and great fights because the enemy of our soul will do all he can to stop us from achieving our goals and vision. Remember that what you embark on is for the glory of God. Come to think about it, God gave Adam and Eve the assignment of accomplishing the mandate that God gave them. Satan, in the form of the serpent, came into the garden to deceive them, and they lost the garden. We must also be very careful to learn from the incident in the Garden of Eden so that we don't become a castaway. There are two incidents that are worth mentioning in this chapter. Samson was born with a sense of duty. He was born with the assignment of what to achieve for his people by destroying their enemies. He was set aside to be a judge and deliverer for his people Israel. However, the enemy created a pitfall in the form of a woman named Delilah.

Judges 16:1-21, King James Version (KJV)

> **1** Then went Samson to Gaza, and saw there an harlot, and went in unto her.
>
> **2** And it was told the Gazites, saying, Samson is come hither. And they compassed him in, and laid wait for him all night in the gate of the city, and were quiet all the night, saying,

In the morning, when it is day, we shall kill him.

3 And Samson lay till midnight, and arose at midnight, and took the doors of the gate of the city, and the two posts, and went away with them, bar and all, and put them upon his shoulders, and carried them up to the top of an hill that is before Hebron.

4 And it came to pass afterward, that he loved a woman in the valley of Sorek, whose name was Delilah.

5 And the lords of the Philistines came up unto her, and said unto her, Entice him, and see wherein his great strength lieth, and by what means we may prevail against him, that we may bind him to afflict him; and we will give thee every one of us eleven hundred pieces of silver.

6 And Delilah said to Samson, Tell me, I pray thee, wherein thy great strength lieth, and wherewith thou mightest be bound to afflict thee.

7 And Samson said unto her, If they bind me with seven green withs that were never dried, then shall I be weak, and be as another man.

8 Then the lords of the Philistines brought up to her seven green withs which had not been dried, and she bound him with them.

9 Now there were men lying in wait, abiding with her in the chamber. And she said unto him, The Philistines be upon thee, Samson. And he brake the withs, as a thread of tow is broken when it toucheth the fire. So his strength was not known.

10 And Delilah said unto Samson, Behold, thou hast mocked me, and told me lies: now tell me, I pray thee, wherewith thou mightest be bound.

11 And he said unto her, If they bind me fast with new ropes that never were occupied, then shall I be weak, and be as another man.

12 Delilah therefore took new ropes, and bound him therewith, and said unto him, The Philistines be upon thee, Samson. And there were liers in wait abiding in the chamber. And he brake them from off his arms like a thread.

13 And Delilah said unto Samson, Hitherto thou hast mocked me, and told me lies: tell me wherewith thou mightest be bound. And he said unto her, If thou weavest the seven locks of my head with the web.

14 And she fastened it with the pin, and said unto him, The Philistines be upon thee, Samson. And he awaked out of his sleep, and went away with the pin of the beam, and with the web.

15 And she said unto him, How canst thou say, I love thee, when thine heart is not with me? thou hast mocked me these three times, and hast not told me wherein thy great strength lieth.

16 And it came to pass, when she pressed him daily with her words, and urged him, so that his soul was vexed unto death;

17 That he told her all his heart, and said unto her, There hath not come a razor upon mine head; for I have been a Nazarite unto God from my mother's womb: if I be shaven, then my strength will go from me, and I shall become weak, and be like any other man.

18 And when Delilah saw that he had told her all his heart, she sent and called for the lords of the Philistines, saying, Come up this once,

THE PITFALLS

for he hath shewed me all his heart. Then the lords of the Philistines came up unto her, and brought money in their hand.

19 And she made him sleep upon her knees; and she called for a man, and she caused him to shave off the seven locks of his head; and she began to afflict him, and his strength went from him.

20 And she said, The Philistines be upon thee, Samson. And he awoke out of his sleep, and said, I will go out as at other times before, and shake myself. And he wist not that the Lord was departed from him.

21 But the Philistines took him, and put out his eyes, and brought him down to Gaza, and bound him with fetters of brass; and he did grind in the prison house.

This is one of the saddest Bible stories I have ever read. Sometimes I read this passage with tears set in my eyes because of the depths of the lesson every achiever must learn. Here is a man who was a child of prophecy, a man whose instruction of birth and growth was delivered by the angel of the Lord. He was born with a clear mission. His mission was to deliver the children of Israel from the hand of the Philistines and their surrounding enemies. He started very well by doing good and bringing deliverance, and the people rejoiced. However, he did not see the pitfall of a vision killer like Delilah, who was bent and determined to destroy him.

We must realize that there will be vision killers and dream destroyers that will serve as pitfalls against us. There will be many Delilahs that we have to watch out

THE PITFALLS

for. These Delilahs are the enemies of our dreams, visions, and our future. We must identify it and avoid it. There are many achievers today that have been slaughtered on the lap of a Delilah somewhere. You must never forget that there is a Delilah for every Samson. For every champion God raises, the devil will try to counter that champion with his own champion. It is my prayer that God will grant you access to divine insight to identify all the pitfalls that have the potential of derailing you from your God-given goals. Sex, money, power, and pride have distracted many from achieving their God-given goals in life. It is very important to watch out for these many pitfalls so that our destiny will not be ruined. Samson was captured by the wicked, his eyes were gouged out, and he became a prisoner in the Land of the Philistines. Even though he ended up killing more people in his death, he is a classical case we can learn a lot from. Never sell your soul out to the devil because of a temporary gain. Never abandon your vision to become a prisoner in the dungeon of Satan.

CHAPTER SEVEN
LASER FOCUS

Focus has always been the mark of an achiever. Everyone that will accomplish their goals in life must have a laser focus. They have to be men and women who will not be easily distracted. Focusing is always paramount and pivotal to the achievement of every goal. Every achiever must have a singular focus on where they are going. Focus is the state or quality of having or producing clear visuals. It is the ability to have a clear-cut vision of where you are going; it is a point of convergence. Focus denotes sharp, crisp, distinct, clear-cut, and well-defined points. As we walk through the journey of life, we must never forget that the goal that we are trying to accomplish is tied to how much focus we have. Our priority will help to determine where our focal point will be. Often, it is that priority that becomes the focal point. The priority does not just become a focal point; it also becomes the fuel that powers our attitude towards our achievements.

It is critical and significant for every achiever to know that the greater their focus, the more they can achieve their goals. Every achiever must focus on the handwork they need to exert to arrive at their goals. It is important to note that no matter how powerful our vision could be, it would amount to nothing if we didn't add handwork.

LASER FOCUS

Every achiever is disciplined with a big focus to major in the major things and, of course, minor in the minor things. The writer of the book Hebrews described the laser focus of Jesus in its chapter twelve rendition.

Hebrews 12:1-6, King James Version (KJV)

> **1** Wherefore seeing we also are compassed about with so great a cloud of witnesses, let us lay aside every weight, and the sin which doth so easily beset us, and let us run with patience the race that is set before us,
>
> **2** Looking unto Jesus the author and finisher of our faith; who for the joy that was set before him endured the cross, despising the shame, and is set down at the right hand of the throne of God.

> **3** For consider him that endured such contradiction of sinners against himself, lest ye be wearied and faint in your minds.

This text is profound in articulating the vision of Jesus and how it serves as a focal point for His sacrifice on the cross. For the joy that was set before Him, He endures the shame of the cross. Every achiever must continually be conscious of their responsibility to remain humble and disciplined towards hard work to achieve their ultimate goal. The path of an achiever is wrapped with a focus on where they are going. It is my prayer that you will have a definite focus on where you are going so that whatever vision God has placed in your heart will become a reality.

CONCLUSION

The path of every achiever is marked by distinctive traits. And these traits characterize the conduit of their progress. This book has highlighted the necessary characteristics an achiever must possess to realize their vision. In chapter one, every achiever must be pregnant with where they are going with their lives. They must be pregnant with what they want to achieve. However, developing a relationship with the Holy Spirit is the only way to have a God-given vision. In chapter two, we discovered that they must not only have visions but also seek how they can interpret the vision. Every vision is for an appointment; therefore, everyone with a vision must seek to know how they can accomplish the vision. Interpreting the vision is seeking to know the strategy of how to convert that vision to reality.

In chapter three, we were able to face the reality of our environment. It is significant to know that the environment of an achiever has a great influence on him. Our environment will determine how far we go with our vision. Every achiever needs a mentor. We saw in chapter four that anyone who will be an achiever must have a mentor to help him. No matter where we want to go, somebody has already been there. There is absolutely no star that stands by itself; every star is a product of another star. Whatever you want to achieve, somebody has done something similar before. All you need to do is ask that person how they did it.

There is a place of sacrifice that every achiever must discover. In chapter five, we discover that the path of an achiever is the path of sacrifice. If we can't pay the necessary price for where we are going, we will be hindered from achieving our goals. However, while we are making the necessary sacrifice for where we are going, we must never forget the many pitfalls we are confronted with on a daily basis. Pitfalls are the hidden danger that we refuse to pay attention to. In chapter six, we explored the many ways we can avoid dream killers and vision destroyers. Focus was a keyword in chapter seven. The path of an achiever is made by laying emphasis on focus. It is the quality of having a clear-cut direction of where we are going. Whatever we want to achieve in life, we must have a strong focus on it. As we walk through the journey of life, having focus will be paramount and a conduit for achieving whatever God has placed in our hearts to do. It is my prayer that as you come to the end of this book, God will grant you continual access to His divine secrets of achievement.

Made in the USA
Columbia, SC
20 June 2023